Unexpected Weather

ABI CURTIS writes poetry and fiction and teaches Creative Writing at the University of Sussex, Brighton, where she also completed a doctorate in Creative and Critical Writing. She won an Eric Gregory Award in 2004 and her work appears in various magazines and anthologies. *Unexpected Weather* is her debut collection and is a winner of the Crashaw Prize 2008.

Also by Abi Curtis

PAMPHLET
Humbug (The Tall-lighthouse)

Unexpected Weather

2008.
Crócigo 2002
Metro 1919.

ABI CURTIS

Sch, 1917.
'Art as technique'
ideas still relevant.

SALT

CAMBRIDGE

PUBLISHED BY SALT PUBLISHING

14a High Street, Fulbourn, Cambridge CB21 5DH United Kingdom

© Abi Curtis 2009, 2011

The right of Abi Curtis to be identified as the
author of this work has been asserted by her in accordance
with Section 77 of the Copyright, Designs and Patents Act 1988.

Salt Publishing 2009
Paperback edition 2011

Printed and bound in the United Kingdom by MPG Books Group

Typeset in Swift 9.5 / 13

ISBN 978 1 84471 565 7 hardback
ISBN 978 1 84471 841 2 paperback

Salt Publishing Ltd gratefully acknowledges
the financial assistance of Arts Council England

1 3 5 7 9 8 6 4 2

for Miles

Contents

Acknowledgements

Acknowledgements are due to the editors of the following publications: 'Mole', 'Bareback Rider', 'Lion Tamer' and 'Hitching' were published in *Magma*; 'Fabric', 'Plastic' and 'Oz' were published in *Succour Magazine*.

'George Gabriel Stokes', 'Rays' and 'Soliloquy of a Molecule' were originally written as part of the 'Motion in Poetry' project at the University of Sussex.

'Bareback Rider', 'Bruise', 'Trapeze Artist', 'Tantric', 'Mole', 'Lupercalia', 'Loom', 'Humbug', 'Electricity' and 'Bean' appeared in the pamphlet *Humbug* (The Tall-lighthouse).

'The Ghost of the Nature Reserve', 'Cloud', 'In-betweens' and 'The Cupboard' (also runner-up in the Essex Poetry Competition, 2004) appeared in the anthology *Seren Selections* by Seren Books.

'The Allotment' and 'Hong Kong' appeared in the anthology *The Allotment* (Stride Books).

'Loom' was a finalist in the Aesthetica Annual Competition 2008.

'Body Baskets' was originally commissioned for *Five: a Book of Art*.

Thanks to those that have supported me during the writing of this collection: The Society of Authors, Sarah Jackson, Roddy Lumsden, Les Robinson, Karen Schaller, Luke Kennard, Andy Brown, Catherine Smith, Nicholas Royle, Paul Myerscough, Julian Broughton, Susan Elderkin, Sam Smith, Anthony Banks, Kim Lasky, my students and, most of all, my lovely family.

I: Fata Morgana

A form of mirage in which images appear in the sky, often inverted or distorted. Named after Morgan le Fey, the sister of King Arthur, who had the power to create such illusions.

Lady Jane Grey
After Paul Delaroche

You saw it when you were a child
and your parents took you to the National Gallery,
up the bank of clean steps and through
the shifting, polished halls.

This was long before we met.
You stood with your thin boy's limbs
before her: Lady Jane, groping
in her blindfold towards the executioner's block.
Your breath stopped.

I saw her years later when I was 16,
about her age, standing on the same spot:
the creamy spillages of silk
that made of her the painting's only
source of light; the lace of her collar against
a white-pink skin of neck, like a lick
of foam clinging for a moment to a swan:

the shadows in the fabric's folds about to drop
and slither back, her fingers reaching for the block
guided by a man in rough fur and black,
her small lips closed as if in sleep.

In the background women swoon,
turning their backs, caressing the grey
bricks. You saw it. You told me:
the executioner cocksure in his red tights,
leaning on the axe, in his face
a kind of love. This death was private,
concealed in the tower from an audience,
but here the bright straw confronts us, spilling

from the canvas, spread like blonde tresses
around the wooden block,
ready to soak in the blood.
According to the books she only panicked once,
crying blindly,
What shall I do? Where is it?
seeking the place to lay her head,
hoping it would be quick. Almost eager.

Once, I didn't know you.
It seems unlikely, unforgivable.
I think of this painting as a portal:
the many shades of grey in the stone background
suggest a staircase, a door, elsewhere.
Wait, show me where to reach my hands.
Wait—
I'm not ready.

Loom

It comes slowly on a web of mist.
Enlarged and indistinct, billowing
on easy gales dropped like stones
through the water of the wind.
It comes slowly through a weave of indigos
and greys, the warp and weft
of the dawn weather,
sliding the sea into the land.
I view the guillemot and wonder,
how *loom* can name its meat,
as well as that which towers over,
that which weaves;
and who might eat a flying thing?
Spread the spindles of its wings,
split its crying beak and glean
only a breast of flesh
from beneath a film of feather.
It comes so slowly
stretching its limits
like milk in a bowl of water.
So slow, it moves backwards.
While I wait, I watch the twist
of a blue-furred caterpillar
inseparable from its own white wires.
The sun shuttles overhead
and as the boat approaches
it shrinks to take an outline that suggests
my dark room turned inside out,
the overlaying drift and push of us,
the reconciliation of our silhouette.

Death by Lightning

I left you in the house, your eyes on me,
suffering from a relative of grief,
took myself from here to the neighbouring village.
I don't usually walk, preferring donkey or moped,
but neither could fare in the weather:
rain slopped from eaves
turning the streets to streams.
Thin fish lost their bearings and followed
to be found tomorrow, breathless,
heads in the railings.
I doubt they knew anything about it,
sent to sleep by strange air lifting their scales.
Rain was in my neck, my boots were buckets,
sky a marbling of dark and unfamiliar faces,
clouds deep as difficult ideas, luminous at their edges.
Light cleaved the sky. I counted and wasn't disappointed
by the sound of a giant piano dropped
onto a collection of empty cauldrons.
I smiled: the sky was furious for me
so I might stay inside the cupboard of my head.
But soon the water overcame, tipping
from flat roofs, stabbing from the arms of lampposts.
Paving slabs lifted to expose whole villages
of slugs and toads.
The sea, two miles away, suggested itself on the wind.
Light revealed a shape at the graveyard gate: a woman under
a yew older than landscape. Room for two. I joined her,
politely distant, staring at the knots and carvings in the trunk:
tracks of every death that's marked elsewhere in stone,
hems of marriages leaving the gate, home for ivy,
sheets of frost and mushrooms shelving out like flesh.
The woman watched the rain as if to concentrate
on just one drop and shuddered when the thunder
spread its voice above the leaves.
She was not beautiful.

She didn't hold her body supple as an animal.
I could not name her type of smile.
Later, I learned she felt the shock in her foot;
shared what I cannot remember.
I looked up through the branches holding
tight their fists of leaves.
I have that image stencilled in my eyelids.
I smelled the metal in the air and tasted
nothing.
You know, if you watch anything through flashes
of lightning, it appears suspended
as if life were frame after frame and never moving.
I was senseless: a snapshot of myself under a canopy.
I'm still here, now in the living room
where we question each other.
I didn't replay memories or gain an answer,
but I've read the best stuff has the power
to take off the top of your head.
You've changed, though you never left this room.
Every day you run your hands over
the root-system printed red on my chest
and in the dark part of your eye
I detect a storm.

In-betweens

I can't help noticing,
tying my shoelaces:
those eyelets let them through.

That's how it is with you.
the soft gap of your mouth,
allowing the traffic

of breaths, whispers and words.
Pinpricks in your ears for
threading lines of silver.

The million lips of pores
are channels for your scent
into the fibres of

your clothes; in turn fastened
through their white button holes:
covering the folded

skin that joins your middle,
vanishing to the star
deep inside your belly.

All this, as you're stretching
to the shelf, sighs living
beside each strand of hair;

fingers slipping a book
into its empty slot,
toes poised on ladder-rungs.

Are the pages settling?
Eyes slide round sockets to
seek me through sifts of dust.

I rise from my lacing,
try to resist blinking
to keep what's between us.

Fata Morgana

From the summit of Elias they saw my dark, elongated towers,
squares of amber light, a hint of a railway, church spires,
hanging in reverse over an indigo of polar sea.
I am a mass of land silent as a whale that features nowhere on the map.
When they returned, I hadn't waited.

I am colder than you think, at the ground.
It matters because what settles above is warm
like the air defying the curve of a valley.
I have the power to change the shapes
of sliding boats: you can never be sure
they will arrive at all.

I don't travel in a straight line, but when you meet my eye
it may as well be a road,
continuous as the future
above which shimmers a promise of water.
Water above which shimmers a promise
continuous as the future;
it may as well be a road
but when you meet my eye, I don't travel in a straight line.

Will they arrive at all?
You can never be sure of sliding boats:
I have the power to change their shapes,
like the air defying the curve of a valley.
It matters because what settles above is warm
and I am colder than you think, at the ground.

When they returned, I hadn't waited.
I feature nowhere on the map; I am a mass of land silent as a whale,
hanging in reverse over an indigo of polar sea:
squares of amber light, a hint of a railway, church spires.
From the summit of Elias they saw my dark, elongated towers.

Body Baskets

Take arms, and after you have wrapped them
about your waist for the last time,
pull them out to leave round red blocks,
empty pockets in a torso.

Coax the glowing optics of veins back through
a needle hole and coil them up neatly,
let them twinkle at you.

Then slide thumbs across your cheeks,
with their brush of roughness.
Pop each chunky digit from its socket.
(Nails may flash their silver coinage.)

Wolf-legs with their wires of hair,
pad up the careful stairs;
wrench hard, then topple them.

Next, sift off milk-film of skins
that lie over the clicking-sticks of bones.
Render them kinetic spares.

With ears that gather whispers,
words mistaken,
the clacket of office chairs,
the shimmy of trains in the rain;
the best thing is to flip them,
live pancakes,
then throw them to the oysters.

The tricky nose with its thousand pickle jars
of wooded walks, of beer-sticky bars,
delicious runway oil, and summer ending,
is best poached,
to turn it white and weary with remembering.

The stomach has done its paunches,
its lunches by streams,
its tumbles in stratospheres of cream,
has felt the touches of cold fingertips
across its uncooked fleshes,
light as a cummerbund.
So forget it.

Turn your attention to
the strawberry-pips of a pair of lips
which follow the circuit of a smile to the Eyes.

Eyes orbit
a delicate root-system of red upon white,
the deep of their windscreens swallowing light,
their waters fledged with cygnets.
Ask them to forgive this,
then blanche them.

The organs are easy,
apart from the queasy second-scent of life
that comes from the lungs:
the last soft wheeze of their inverted trees.

The heart's not as difficult as you might expect,
just a bubble of thick fibres,
just the four-wheel driver
of everything.

Come close and blood's
no liquid but a fleet of boats,
skimming the labyrinth.
And closer still the atom spins
back to itself,
unravelling each filament it finds

as though no more than the light
of a long-gone constellation,
or the frayed ends of a ball of twine.

George Gabriel Stokes

stands upon the Giant's Causeway watching
Atlantic breakers shape and remake

whites and greens and slatey-blues.
Clouds answer by opening and bunching like hands
possessed by a wind that tunnels as blood

through the dark artery of headland.
He has taken long strides over columns
of cooled lava and returned

to this place beneath a storm.
Some believe the Causeway is the work of Finn McCool
in fierce wrangle with a giant Scot
crashing his feet until Benbulben reeled.

George remembers Mary, tired at the stove:
astronomer's daughter who replaced his God.
Her skin puckered at the belly for what she gave,
but nothing more than that to show:

two, the little girls, just stilled like unwound clocks;
one, the boy, a doctor, pushed morphine through his blood—
too much. An accident.
Then something else replaced his God:

George thought of platelets spinning in the body's liquid,
of vortices living off the height of tall and taller buildings,
a tear, close-up, re-shaped by breath upon it.

He looks at Dundee Castle, East Portrush, leaning
at the lip of rock. There was a violent storm here once
that forced the falling of the kitchen

with a scatter of cooks and cookware across
the bleak, hexagonal cubes into the broil below.
George Stokes observes the turning sea, lost
in calculations and a drifting thought

of Claude Navier, thinking the same before him;
building bridges at Asnières, Choisy,
suspended over the Seine,
watching the hulls of boats churn up the calm.

The Navier-Stokes equations are used to understand motion in gases and
liquids.

Soliloquy of a Molecule

I am moving here, through & over
colliding into time and more time.
All of us: vibrations and interactions.
We circle.
We straight-line.
I am nothing and then something and then substance.
I can't tell where I am: at the bottom? Or up above?
Someone is flying underneath me, or looping over.
I could be slowed and gentled. I can be fostered.
I can be bullied and outnumbered. I'll go over there.
Wherever that is. With the others, along with them.
Working all the time against them.
I dislike all of them.
You've got to love them.
Zoom me closer. Take me to the edge.
Hoist me back.
Lead me to the middle where I'll watch
from an eye our gathering makes.

We move so quickly, I cannot see us.
Like we're going somewhere.
Like peas in a sorting machine. A trillion marbles dropped
from a cliff. But not solid or fixed. Invisible.
We have our language. Spin us fast enough in the guise of ink:
we'll form arabesques only we can decipher.
We don't have skill or art but we are all elegance.
We're watching for something to resist us,
bring us back to ourselves.
We are each other, without souls.
We change locations, meshing like ghost-skin then melting again.
We are the simple dissolution of our own mind.
We sing.
I sing.

Trapeze Artist

My calf-muscle encircles the cloud-ring.
I coil the ropes,
looping my limbs on the push-pole.
Wear an elephant hair at your wrist.
Don't whistle in the dressing-room.
In the circus, accidents happen in threes.

My hands condense to a squirrel's grip;
I grow a pendulum to lend me gravity.
The danger of our mass is what we share:
as you lengthen into nothing,
I must ground my toes against the air.

Each catch of sinews is
a work of chance.
I trust your long fingers,
though they don't know me.
You grip my ankles in the netless dark,
turning the sawdust ring
into my altitude.

At close, when the windjammer hangs
his music on the peg,
and the rigging's coiled slackly round the tent,
I press my hensile toes into grass
damp and flossed with cigarettes,
watching the swing of your skeleton.

On the ground, you anchor your life to another,
arm resting like weather across her shoulders.
Every moment standing witness to
your four feet stepping slow,
will bring me closer
to vertigo.

Lupercalia

This is a night to go out.
Dare the wolves to circle.
Beyond the fire their eyes
uncountable
Beyond those, breathing rolls back
to a forest of firs
shaped as the flights of arrows.

This is a night to go out
Put on layers and layers
Keep your own warmth close
Don't envy fire in any window
Swivel your ears
to the noises you love
Keep low
Take your leave.

This is the night to go out.
Your shoulders roll towards
the Prussian blue of later
the soft-spots of an old dusk
the tender fury of clouds.
Follow this logic and

hours from now, you'll witness
a marriage in the alleyway
six eyes telling you
Keep our secret, we have our reasons
You circle them
Lope to where there's room
to view approving looks
from the moon.

This is the night you'll end up
calling through the o-shaped valve
of the throat, long and loud
until everything's connected
The night you won't remember how
you made it home
or got like this:
smoky and besotted.

Hong Kong
For Simon

I was a gwailo, waiting on the harbour-front, buttoned-up in itchy green. No doubt, the sweat drawing its way down my starched collar smelt to others of milk and butter. Junks dunked in the brown water, lit up from above by dragons of neon. Evil spirits were being dashed off feng shui buildings, deflected into the sweet stench of the South China, smoothed over by the ferryman. The sweep of the science building was a cornet of shells. I looked into a window, transparent blue. The same colour as my eyes. And saw you, leaning to the light, standing in the lab, coated in white; a sanitised angel. You squinted at little phials of gold liquid, held them up to the dropping dim sum of the sun. I had journeyed all my life to see this: your flat frown through a window. I had been a thin white dog, lost within the cardboard streets of the walled city. I had walked the Des Voeux Road, meeting pith-helmeted men in the Old Gloucester Hotel, breathing the rot of blue eggs boiled behind doorways. I had lived with Salisbury Row's clammy touches to my silver buttons, stumbling across Blake Pier, coming up for air to watch ladders rise from the water. All for this: my feet crossing from Tsim Sha Tsui, you viewing the urine samples of strangers, catching my stare and flicking the blinds shut. My lungs felt bashed by a cricket bat.

But later, as the spores began to swell in their humid petri-dish, you sought me out with my sun-burnt scalp, taking my arm, trying your mouth on stretched English vowels. We found our scrap of gold along Nathan Road, and kept a stone frog at the windowsill. That way, we stayed together when the little red book went off like a bomb, laying low 'til Deng swept in with the monsoons, washing everything in sideways rain.

The plane takes us out, touching cheongsams drying on the precarious threads between buildings. The city expands hourly into the sky, and it takes time to climb high enough to leave. You've never seen the clouds like this: clean. To you, they have been scrubbed and softly brushed. They are all around us now, resting on the hills. They smell of pine and rabbits' fur.

Rays

We took the blue stairs down below the edge of the Thames
into the aquarium, where the world's oceans are boxed
and all light is the same hue covering us.
We shouldn't be here. Or they shouldn't.
Benthic. Dragged up from continental shelves.
The soft, living fossils of sea-horses,
melancholy as questions.
Huge fish with the faces of people we once knew:
geography teachers, uncles, dentists,
expressionless, sliding onwards ignorant of glass.
Which side of the window?
The sharks don't answer, their tails have a different grammar;
nothing like our lumbering moves.
They are feeling for electrical fields
or one part per million of blood,
showing us their beautiful teeth.
I smile at you, behind the camera. No flash:
it damages their lidless eyes, their flesh.
Later, when I look, I am all darkness,
a shape on the sea's surface.

By now we have forgotten daylight
and watch the filaments of jellyfish,
retaining a trace inside our eyelids.
Beyond the deeper tunnels are rays in an open pool,
their heads continuous with pectoral fins,
themselves continuous with chill water.
We roll sleeves up and they offer
their furled edges to our touch.
They feel like thickened water,
dusted, as with flour.
We know that if they're felt too often
pink lesions show on their mottled backs:
we would take something from them,
their coating, their boundary.

And still they offer themselves
like us to each other,
fingerprints all over,
flat, rolling children who believe
they move the oceans.

Tantric

We moved across long sands
and light-heavy lakes in the direction
of an outrage.

We learned that there are many kinds of embrace
One like the mixing of sesamum with rice

One where the kind of love
combines milk with water
or twines as a creeper
judging between too tight and not tight enough.

You tell me the rain here makes your thoughts smaller
as you watch its yellow drops fall beyond the veranda.

They are as big as teacups, filtered through heat and green.
You're quiet. Not like me; I want dialects
moving through me, the alien shapes of lips
in running rivulets of Hindi and Sanskrit.

More: I want to be inhabited.
We learned different kinds of contact. My favourite is the pressed kiss.
We must get this right, like the line of your neck: precise.
We must convert language into the correct quietness.

I've read myself in the Valley of Scinde
under the blue mountains where the falcon slips
between one round thought and one with razor-edges.
I'll compress the travel of my mind into a sutra.

I'm thinking of the Haj, the square of black that lived
in my stomach while I waited and walked, dousing

my deep sin in zemzem.
I pretended all trades and named myself
Mirza of Bushehr, to be mastered
by something heavier than pilgrims.

I loomed behind your slim silence,
turned to groundwork and powdery tea, spent

warped time with the tantras.
Each is something other than their instruction,
warning I might scar my face on the native's javelin
and go unrecognised along the brown Nile as I would in London.

You have long fingers that roll over the paper.
You hear the little machines of the Sanskrit.
They look like spinning wheels or trees
but translate from theory into flesh.

I can speak them down from my palate,
from the loss that opens the part of my throat
I didn't know I had.

Cloud

Before we could travel by air
we knew them only as
the grubby underbellies of giant,
white cats.

But now, above them, on the other side,
I think differently of ground:
dense, silted, packed with sediment,
the opposite of cloud

with its haberdashery of vapours,
so tactile, so sure of itself.
A piping of white confidence.
Stackings without shelf.

It can't be negotiated by any
human digit,
does not belong to us but to beings
formed boneless

who share the sky but
are invisible to our bolshy eyes,
so weightless their weightlessness
itself escapes us.

They design their villages
to shift their driftings,
tread a strange foundation—
not on or in or under
but *with* the cumulus,

their disappearings,
their accumulations.

Hitching

She was in an ice-cream mood,
having escaped the motorway,
watching it from the B-road until
it folded back into two dark fronds
like a pioneer's moustache.
She didn't have much:
two issues left of a subscription,
a chunk of April wrapped
in the pocket of her pack,
and a sandwich of mustard cress.
She counted telegraph poles all the way back
to a town strung with three-hundred lanterns.
Not her town, but a place that smelt sweet
as the absence left by bark torn from a tree.
A deer greeted them as they took the turning;
leisurely, welded to shadow. They braked hard.
A fingerprint of light on the windscreen.
She made a note for her chronicle.
The driver watched.
We know a little about her.
About us: she knows a lot.

Last Words from the Bluebird

The grey-green hills hang above the water and wonder *where is he?*
Deeper than miles down. They hold the memory of the last moment.
More than 300 miles an hour. The fastest over lake or river
a bird of steel had been.

He speaks to them through the ricochet
Out-running time and the reeling clouds
Coniston's breath smoothing the depths.

I can't see much.
The water's very bad indeed.
I'm getting a lot of bloody row in here.
I've got the bows up.
I'm gone.

We think about that last game of solitaire:
drawing an ace then a queen of spades.
Adjustments on the instruments.
A perfect day. Two perfect runs.
But never fast enough.
What could he say when the instant came?
The water listens, plays back.

I can't see much.
The water-balance is very brackish indeed.
I'm getting a lot of blooming rowans in the hereafter.
I've got the bow-bearer in here.
I'm on the gong.

Who knows what happens when you reach top speed.
Does time take you?
Do you stay with it through thirty-odd years
And speak?

I can see music.
The water is very wrong and unfeasible.
Iambics are gathering rowdy blossoms in here.
It's gothic in the bower.
I know I'm good.

They found him after a long sleep
dressed in his nylon suit on the lake-bed.
Should we have left him in the bluebird's final flight
Shattering over the broken water
Speaking still across it?

I'm the cantilever.
That waul I gave was wrung from me indecently.
Iciness on the gauge. I'm for rubber-necking in here.
Gouging the H_2O with the bow-head.
I'm gulped up and not returning.

Listen, listen: that's what the green-grey hills would say,
If only they could.

II : Ignis Fatuus

A phosphorescent light seen hovering or flitting over marshy ground.

"This impression seene of the land, is called in Latine ignis fatuus, foolish fire, that hurteth not but only feareth fooles."

— WILLIAM FALKE, 1640

Mole

Velour glove with no fingers.
Earth's secretary,

shoving on,
I coax the ground to follow.

My middle-ear a curve of bone
brokering the sighs of worms,

glad knees of brittle crickets,
lady-spiders tapping their heels

impatient for the sun's thump
as it spooks up by increments.

I build a supple chimney
for a fossil's hearth,

pulse a code
along the vertebrae

instructing the secretion
of biography.

Crisp delicacy of wings,
juicy pips of insect eyes:

my slow food, on the move
I clean my whiskers on the malachite.

I'm an initiate, I know
the hue of beetroot by my taste buds,

can sniff the difference at dawn,
the peaty tang of dusk,

sound-out the déjà vu
of constellations,

identify the clues that lace
the rain's low conversation.

I work alone, rowing the bones
to hold apart a way home.

You misconceive,
I don't intend to use it:

I look back only once
(so to speak)

clearing the road of molecules
for your return.

You'll pull the file,
delve the archive

then come scooping
through the loam.

The very moment you have proved me,
is the one I'll make you mine.

Tyndall's Flame

I am a stranger in town gathering with a crowd
in the lecture hall. The benches give and creak
like bones. A smell of smoke, cologne and clay.

He takes the stage with a Bunsen-burner
and draws from it the tallest flame, brimming
blue, flecked with greens and browns

like the inside of an eye. I watch.
A flame is a tulip; it bows and whispers.
Tyndall speaks to us and lets us wonder.

He'll show the nervousness of flames:
Their sensitivities and starts and foibles.
A flame is a person; a friend, your family.

A flame is a lip. A bud. My nightmare.
I watch. A woman in the front row knits.
Fire catches in her irises like knots.

He'll demonstrate enigmatic resonance
to each of us. To all. The blaze roars
like a human enraged.

Tyndall sings his fire-tune.
It prisms, flourishes and turns.
It looks to be in pain and trying

to escape. I don't feel well or right.
A flame is a picture. An orange-rind.
A flame is a quick thought of red.

recover sensation
of life.

in mechanical
~~world~~ century.
world.

ce. The cliff-edge.
d as a broken egg. 3 poems.
me to the beat of a watch.

from the audience
:thing runs over my body,
as if a man could turn tuning-fork.

I zing.
I quiver.
Rare as a letter.
Sore as flame over droplets of water.

Don't make a sound.

But he leaves the room and whistles
from a closed apartment three stories away
and the flame twists on its plinth.

A flame is deep pain in the faces around me.
I shall jig over the rooftops until I'm out of air.
To think: I only came in here to escape the rain.

Criticises idea of Adrian Mitchell "
– most people ignore most poetry –
– not it made fashionable
by defam –
– interesting –
state poem

conc... defam suggests ~~structure~~ system of lit
changes over time by absorbing what may seem
out of fashion and making it the new fashion –
new way of viewing life depending on how
modern life is, small things increasingly
go unnoticed.

S's model of defam works from the
classical structuralist notion that
[36] "structure is a closed system,
changing by realigning its parts rather than
introducing something new"

Bruise

Today, a thought cut down
by a slip on a wet drain
sending flesh to crack against tarmac,
a thigh smarting on impact.

Later, twisting into a thin mirror
I see the swell, veins shattering the surface.

Tomorrow, a head-sized bruise
the colour of bears on asphalt,
its edges spread like the belly of a storm cloud.

A charcoal rubbing: it shows my white
webbings of growth, my mishap
a spillage of ink across a blotter.

And the day after, as though a slip
of water had dissolved its line
to petrol-green, broils of blue,
at its centre a violet-maroon

which, from a certain distance, is the felt
on a doe's flank as she lies at the roadside,
her eyes black lights in the blackberry hedge,
her breathing velvety, insistent.

[37]

Handwritten annotations:

mimesis
art imitates / that it / describes

poem style to replicate detail of bruise on impact of the fall skin of the fall

shop + memory

impact the sensation of falling / bruising

inconsistent line length, no fluency of the bruise — like development of the bruise

uncomfortable

enjambment

imagery all ugly — lexical field appropriate — doesn't stray far from subject matter — impact?

title — simplistic — poem (body of) itself explores this through imagery — makes the tone ironic.

form / flow of poem mimics bruise — deepen — refreshes our perspective

The Cupboard

. . . the word-hoard is not a cupboard . . .
— NORTHROP FRYE

A tile of light lifts
a shift of onion skins aside.

Potatoes, nobbled with time,
rock forward as giant toes,
earless but listening

to lids click,
and a spider spangling her lines of thought:
a twist of white between
the wood and where it splits.

A crane fly, startled he's alive,
tiptoes the toolbox,
risking his fragility on nails and wires
menacing to himself.

Dropping slowly from the shelf
he leaves

a leg behind:
a pencil-mark, an underline.

The spider trawls him.
Then with herself she quickly sews him:
a thin of wings,
a mess of legs,
wrapped and over-wrapped in threads.

A duster turns a feather,
recalling flight and water,

while the spider
finishes her package
then stacks it neatly
with the others.

Plastic
after Ovid

She is impressionable: cellulose and camphor, and I will have her.

She's found ways to elude me, circumstances bend around her. The streets are sometimes like a movie-set: walls-on-wheels roll out in the path of my chase, concealing her as she ticks through the streets.

When I first saw Daphne, it was from the front. She was unkempt: long knots of hair twisting around her neck, a sweater with a pulled thread, flaky skin. I wanted to cultivate her, gloss her with pro-vitamins. We talked for a while. Her dialogue was difficult to follow — too dense. Now and then she'd tip in a bowlful of laughter. My eyes were all over. With them, I thumb-rolled her supple pores, lingered over her cheek-apples, drew the soap-stone line of the jaw. I admit I was disappointed when she turned sideways against the bar for another gin and tonic. Her profile was not so pleasing. Her nose had a lump at the top the shape of a seed-pod or beach pebble. It turned down too: a vole's droop, I thought; a water-heavy laurel. I wanted her even more. I have the means to perfect her.

I come from a deep ancestry. I look nothing like Sashrata who lived almost a hundred generations before me. He worked beside the grey Ganges, repairing the chopped noses of the punished. A leaf-shaped skin-flap peeled from the cheek, the twist from the septum to show the underside iridescent with capillaries. I looked at the gin's transparent slip in the glass and wondered what spirit Sashrata used to loose-limb his patients. I smelled the sweet-black of powdered liquorice, red stains of sandalwood, barberry, sesame oil. Such different pigments and aromatics; not like ethanol and bleach. All laid out to dust and slick the wounds, as an artist prepares his mixes for a portrait. The slim curve of hawkbill forceps. A slither of razor-sharpness like a fine brush.

I wanted to tell Daphne of his workshops, how students practised incisions in the swollen abdomen of a watermelon, of bone-repair on cracked earthenware, blood-stemming accomplished on reeds weeping sap. But she wouldn't understand.

We'd been together for seven months before I broached the subject. By then she bloomed with a dusting of powder and her hair held the light. I placed myself squarely in front of her as often as I could. When I did view her from the side, I'd map my cuts. She liked my cupped hands at her neck, holding her head like a prize. She'd close her eyes. But when I finally asked her if she'd let me complete her beauty, she left. It had just been raining and the street was a thin shine, her reflection chaperoning her through the wet.

When I catch her there will be change. I know her, she loves me. She will agree. It will be this easy: I'll press the tears away and set to work. Her heart will be wrapped in a new, monitored sleep. Her gown will be green. I will take my instruments and pare the excess away. Like bark.

Lion-Tamer

I wear a white suit:
skin-tight, rhine-stoned.
The audience always gasp:
imagining he attacks me,
raising red muscles to a human-stand.
But it is love that trembles over,
its claws steadying my small shoulders.

I wear a white suit:
so his passion is invisible,
my scars, covered.
Yes, I've come close enough—
in the past they've turned and ravaged me,
finding themselves back in that never-known dust,
lusty for munch of bone and suck of silk.
My white suit should be barred with black.

I love him more than any man.
At night I rest my head and hands
in his dangerous halo,
breathing the musk of blood and dung.
Every evening after the come-in,
after the slap of the switch,
when the sloping prowl begins,
He eyes me up,
then the white lines that remember him
ache to be reopened.

Poem at the Edge of a Cliff

look up a-height. The shrill-gorged lark so far
Cannot be seen or heard. Do but look up.
— *King Lear*, ACT IV, SCENE VI

She has not worried over coming to this place
to treasure the air and stand
heels lifting on the grass, the camber of her brain
resetting itself. It isn't difficult to look
down or out to the hard sea, its water stilled
by this height, waves peaking and toppling

invisibly on themselves. She imagines her body's topple
should she overbalance, leaving this place
for another, her flight stilled
for a moment by the dreadful air's last stand.
Up here, on the careful verge, she looks
free enough, a walker with breezes through her brain

following the idle fires of thought, the brain's
own jumps as it accepts the toppling
difference between dry land and sea, the look
of light on each of them. It keeps their places
where she would swap them. She cannot stand
the boundaries, and rocks and wavers but still

cannot give up the way the earth holds still.
She longs for the small, halfway-down moment, her brain
figuring it as worthy trade, a moment to stand
alone in time, the bottom of the top
that would make it worth the maps and hike to find this place.
She sits and rests her head upon her hands, looking

like a rolled-up statuette, casting her looks
to the choughs that bounce and drift, are never still.
The coolness of the grass seeps into the secret places
of her skin, she thinks of this as a last touching, her brain
registering the thrill of feeling, on top
of the limit of the land where the body takes its stand.

She stretches out her arms to grab the standing
air and all the edges freeze as if to look
at her braced body, not yet gone but toppling
through the gull's shed feathers and stockstill
rocks. Thoughts loosen as her brain
is released from all its casings to fill new places.

She can no longer look to see the top
still there, her brain has lost old thoughts
and all the places they have ever stopped and stood.

Bareback Rider

There is nothing better or worse
than a horse. I tightrope
on Appaloosa stepping stones
set in a back of dusted hair,
feel the muscles meld with my own.
Tuned into hamstrings,
my flat foot to a deltoid,
dappled in the shadows
of a safety net,
my girl's body dazzles
with machinery of heft and bone.
I'm spread thin at my extremities,
my eyes equine and hooded.
We go, transforming sawdust
to a sea's rough shoreline,
drumming light through it.

While we are one, we are safe.
But an errant fingertip,
a turn of eye a millimetre left,
a camera-flash might spook
a tendon out of synch.
And then we'll know the hooves,
the drop down to
the smack of shit and confetti
on the lips. The taste
of tigerclaw and clownfoot.

There'll be a strange perspective on
the pinnacle of silk that forms a roof.
I'll see the grimace of the ringmaster
upside down in my disaster:
my pearlescent taffeta spattered,
breathing wetly,
untethered, untamed;

her feather slumped, eyes garish.
He'll lift me to my shuddered feet
to bow, remount and flourish.

Tonight I'll think of her tied and trussed,
only tarpaulin and grass between
my chilly flesh and her twitching flank,
picturing how a simple slip
might be enough to free us.

Michelangelo's Meals

For the fig bread. Under the head, which speaks.
— MICHELANGELO

For food, he pays in poems.
He tells of winter flowers folding.

For thoughts on death he eats ripe melon, thick wine, olives
moving over themselves. He gives knowledge,

calling his payments *squibs*; minuscule explosives
yielding packages of breads and cheeses.

His stomach stretches, his hand spreading
over strips of paper that curl like butter.

Heaven is no more or less than greens or pickled trout
and loves are meats with too much pepper or without.

Here he lies sleeping as the acids are digesting,
pulping what he's chewed to letters.

From under those he wakes and finds the bloom on grapes
then opens it to cloud-hung purple lakes.

The Ghost of the Nature Reserve

They found my body here;
where dandelion clocks tick,

counting the years in airborne wishes.
There is nothing more delicate than this,

Except for eyelashes
closed forever in the nettles

or miniature fingers clamped tight in the chaff,
shreds of a stranger's skin in their beds.

I melted slowly into soil;
food for woodlice, their caresses coiling

through my hair, streaked in silver
every evening by star-shine and snails,

but left alone by moths in their flimsy dresses;
they search for light elsewhere.

Owl Butterfly

Idle on a round leaf
it shows its unseeing amulet:
an owl's look printed as a masquerade
on a ragged wing the hue of tree-skin.

It rests folded in a warm glass house
behind the vast, tapestried palace
we visited to celebrate the two of us.
We have been startled out of ourselves.

Owl-mask carried lightly as a paper kite
by this spindled insect whose own fractured
seeing eye's more blind somehow
than the painted pupil that reflects us

knowing it will never swoop the vistas
of the palace, cheat its labyrinths,
or perch upon the shoulder of a statue
in the dark long after closing time.

It will only look after us
as the lights snap off,
and then gaze beyond the glass
opening out the revelation of its other half.

The Allotment

Look for it here:

Follow the blackberried track to where
shallots and violets reek their invites.

Unlock the gate that breaks the morning's
spider's web, letting
parsnip-tips receive their droplets.

These boots, forever moulded to your toes,
stand in line with queues of rhubarb.

Gently brush the furled kale,
Fall in love with veined greengages:
rain bubbles solidified

to flesh, their globular heads
amongst the buttered lettuce.

Wigwams of lanky broad beans,
white hot, red-dipped radishes,
muscled spinach give

as you lift the mole-black soil
and ease them to your barrow.

You will not find the answer here

Or in the quick flick of a rabbit's tail,
startled by its own curved image
in the pendulous drag of damsons.

Or in uneven squares of plots,
Dapper scarecrows, copper taps,

Or in the field below the slope
where year-old horses chase
themselves along the fences.

For there is nothing of it here.

You can watch a marrow loom
from lithe courgette
to grotesque thumb,

Or pull apart an artichoke:
One tubular heart, one bulbous choke.

But look close

Along your sun-dried arm,
your nails bedded with wet earth,
the flaked handle of a trowel or fork

Twisting in the mulch and worms.
Find, among each sift and turn,

walk-less husks of millipedes
and unforgiving knots of weed;
This is where you'll learn.

Mycelium

The dusk opens up and we take torches, searching
for mushrooms: fruit bodies in crowded clusters,
cross veins and candle snuff. We are recovering
from an argument, among moss in wet acid grassland
where the Shaggy Earth Tongue chatter,
where fungi no bigger than matchsticks
pop from leaf litter in pitch dark woodland,
where the slender white stems gather,
and the Bell Cap bleeds in the peaty soil.

We have been here in early mornings
in good mood and found species
delicately-fleshed and not highly recommended;
inedible or grooved and better when slow-cooked.
Our field guide crinkled in the damp
listing the round or oval caps,
depressed centres, creamy browns,
crowded gills, curls and parasols.

Now our lights braille across soft-bodied forms
not readily given to the process of fossilisation.
Your eyes shine as the sun shrivels. You read to me:
Beware highly poisonous lookalike Livid Entoloma.
I know all things are not what they seem.
Each of us has a double to catch in our hat,
thriving near swamps, buried wood, gardens, parks
and even pavements. An Amethyst Deceiver.

You point, excited, forgiving me. I take
the twizzled stem, flake the mealy-smelling meat.
By deep night we've spotted flat, moist, slate-blue caps,
a Wood Woolly-Foot clinging like character to dead leaves,
an intermission of Silky Nolareas, The Miller, leathery and neat.
The margin of the morning brings needles underfoot,

an open flask, a crop of Dead Man's Fingers. A brush of hands,
the unfurling of a grass-lit hill, showing the way
like a root-made web to the insubstantial roof
above our bed.

Electricity

VOLTA

You four good souls will help me show them.
Hold this moist zinc, bring your finger to his tongue-tip.
Sir, in turn gently touch the third's eyeball.
This contact feels unusual.
Third man: damp your hands and hold
this gutted mouse. Then number four, share
the carcass in your right and grasp tight
this shining sheet of silver in your left.
Perfect, making sure your palms are wet.
Let me check us. Now we're ready.
Touch the silver to our first man's zinc—
Yes! You feel it? A bitter taste for you.
A flash of light upon the other's eye.
The creature flickers though he's lifeless,
joined between your fingers.
With this I show what flows between us
needs dissimilarity. Your tongue and my fingertip
swarm with our differences.

AMPERE

His father tasted acid when the guillotine fell.
So he wondered then about metals and parallels.

He proposed to Julie and expected 'no' because
His words meant every meaning's loss.
She said otherwise, but died in the distance
stretching from Bourg to Poleymieux.
Then a vacuum formed.

He proposed for magnetism,
small circuits inside a substance,
waves for the passage of light,
the distance between a pair of infinite conductors,
but failed to explain how the experiments
that proved the rule could not have inspired it.
Or why he wrote his diary in the third person,
recounting how he imagined
someone being there
to touch her dead eyes shut.

OHM

This blind moment is made by the flash
of an ice skate.
At university, I neglected my studies,
preferring the switchblade circles of my waltz
across a frozen lake, the same turns
in the waxed dance hall, hands encircling a waist,
the invisible lines and arcs a billiard ball made.
The friends, the wine, the laughs. I paid
with my career, in the sure sphere of recognition.

Even when I sought to demonstrate the ratio
of potential difference between a conductor—
I forget . . . it had to do with currents . . . close contacts . . .
So what did I know? Nothing, after all,
but I got that chair of physics two years before I died.
My memory holds a creature trapped beneath the ice.

HARRY

Did he twitch, or fizz, or violently convulse,
his hair strung out in shocks of blame?
How did he make his bold escape?
How could a hamster tolerate such high voltage
through his tiny frame? The street lights popped.
A heart as big as a bean shoot stopped.
A little girl was sent to bed distraught.

The house was silence that night.
A secret struggle pried the rodent from his wire grip.
The silk bundle of his fur was bedded in sawdust
to await a twilight burial beneath wet grass.

A new evening swung itself around the house
drawing headlights through the garage door,
picking out the edges of a creature
clattering around a wheel as if
he were powering back up.
As if to weave silver.

Humbug

The first time we saw him I was small enough
to examine gaps in the paving slabs
see luggage of moss and insect husk:
a broth of ghosts moving there and back.

He appeared stuck to the foot
of the house, mistaken for button or sweet
encased by a spirally line of my thought
from body of stone to heart of meat.

I was taken in before the dark curved over.
I woke to the mail sliding in with the sun.
Humbug had crept to the height of my shoulders
lugging his hollow house along mine.

The rain brought its wet machine.
The slimed glass had me captured
in a casement of low, vibrating tones
I imagined had come from the future.

The sun climbed in and

Humbug had scaled higher. It was for me
one wet muscle went, bringing
his clockface to the rooftop,
eyes like victory-fingers.

I called on orange-haired Frazer
to show how Humbug upended horizons.
We came in slow motion through the gate
saw triangles set in a black paving stain

No Humbug where he should have been.
The murmur of the rain began like quiet terror.
The black stain and my Humbug were the same:
creeping, quiet shells that stick and shatter.

Oz

She wanted to go home and I wanted to take her
but she found me first, propped on a pole,
coated in shady crows all pluck-plucking
at my straw stuffing.
I had forgotten how to think,
my skull an empty pumpkin on a stick;
an empty nest within.
I'm dry, I told her, I haven't had a drop in years.
She smiled thinly, dusting off her dress.
I followed her because I longed for marrow:
some convoluted mass of foldings that might
put me in touch with her skin and my skin.
The road slid on, its pointing gone, the mortar crumbling.
I creaked and shifted through. She stepped,
click-clacking over the cracks.

Out came the woodsman, rusty tin can from the trees.
We hadn't met in years, but something about her
brought him on with a scraping sound. Unbearable:
hollow echo of contractions and dark chambers.
She dripped thick oil on his joints.
I remember it like amber: yellow blood of secrets.
He thanked her and we eyed each other,
both after what she had inside: the pulsings of a spirit.
If we were rivals, there was nothing in it.

Her sorrow drifted us to the matted fur of a lion.
We were alarmed at first but he was shrinking
in the crackled grasses, stinking of meat and fear.
She was persuasive and he followed like a giant dog:
a washed out sandpit with paws.
He told us he was lacking courage, had no inclination.
No surprise, we thought, and let him join us.

We read the papers on the way and then I ate them.
Tin would whittle sticks and set my teeth on edge.
We groomed Lion before bed.
There were some scrapes with drooping, poisoned poppies,
wolves and drumming bees and winged monkeys,
but still we made it.

When we reached the wizard he appeared
as something else to each of us;
to her, a massive head with great green eyes, she said.
To Tin: a beast with ravenous, corrosive teeth.
Lion saw a burning ball of flame to cook him in.
To me, the vision of a woman more beautiful than any.
A woman who can kill with water.
A woman looking for the strangeness of home.

While I slept, in my parched dream
I felt that I was him: small, wizened,
lost in a ballooning incident, embarrassing.
Capable of migraine, heart murmurs and acts of bravery,
with the aid of a mirror, projectors and a screen.
I woke to all kinds of wings and teeth,
back on my pole, surrounded by tall crops
and long streaks of rain.

My chest is pounding, my temples thrumming
and I've a mind to start moving again.

Roundhouse

They travelled Bodmin moor
seeking the house without lines
watched by square-toothed ponies from the woods.

Their taxi rolled through shallow mires,
black, incongruous against the wilful heather.
Each fell in love with the silence.

A dwelling without corners.
A return to the site of their birth.
Barely a shade of thought between these daughters.

In the home with nowhere the devil may lurk
is a perfect curve to steal a voice
and send it back as no longer yours.

This isn't all they heard:
granite chitter slipping along the path,
the creak as the table began to turn,

lining up the railway from porch to hearth
and Mother's portrait sliding sideways
to the route that's coming around.

Mandibles

For Sarah J.

The archaeologists have been in the office again.
You've come to work through the night when

you find their shoeboxes shelved with the books,
then face the other way, try to write, to look

at the dark-glazed view into the quad.
You turn around, fingering the lip of a box.

Nobody said, *Don't Touch*. This one's labelled
MANDIBLES. As you slide the lid, a smell

of dried mouths and subtle rot.
Each piece of jaw in a plastic pocket

you can feel through to the nubs of bone,
unable to identify symphysis, molar, canine.

You recall Mr Fozard pulling a tooth
to leave a hole for your tongue to search, a taste

of pink, of omnivore. Bridges, dentures,
ivory tusks cross sectioned

like the rings of an oak;
pulp canals, the roots that bind your mouth

to your thinking head.
Porcelain, amalgam, gold:

offerings to the speech of the soul.
But here, in this box, the bones are small,

herbivorous. At last you see animals,
re-skinned and furred, decay reversed,

their skulls re-clothed:
deer stripping red fruit from the hedgerow,

rabbits, lightheaded and wet-eyed,
clipping the green from the fields.

Bean

The garden's plush with acorn husks,
pears like dropped bells,
apples, bareheaded in the grass.
My two-year-old toe curls

like my mother's,
and my grandmother's woven herself
through the wool of my hat:
knit one, purl one. Her daughter unpicks

the seam of a gone-to-seed runner bean,
revealing four ovules.
Organ-shaped, they gleam
the barely-pink of an eye-white.

What are they? She explains
the gloss of their bodies,
how each can be buried:
a capsule descending

Earth's pocket
to reach a sticky fist back up,
pointing out the apple tree.
Look. Watch:

if I could travel fast enough,
I'd catch light sleeping
under the sofa, I see
misshaped beads, strings cut,

clinking: a game of marbles,
each encasing a morula.
I expect a fine fuzz along the wallpaper,
a leguminous smell from green Lego.

Even now,
the sky's segmented hull
is podded with rooftops
and unexpected weather.